A SCRIPTURAL ROSARY – 1596

PETER HUYCK

A Scriptural Rosary – 1596

ST PAULS

For Domenicus Prutenus (d.1460)

ST PAULS Publishing
Morpeth Terrace, London SW1P 1EP, U.K.

Copyright © ST PAULS 1999

ISBN 085439 572 5

Set by TuKan, High Wycombe
Produced in the EC
Printed by AGAM

St Pauls is an activity of the priests and brothers
of the Society of St Paul who proclaim the Gospel
through the media of social communication

Contents

The Glorious Misteries

Foreword

Scriptural rosaries have become increasingly
popular; nearly thirty new ones have appeared since
John Gabriel published *Scriptural Rosary* in the
United States in 1961. One of the best was published
over four hundred years ago at an illegal press in
England, at a time when carrying a rosary was
proscribed by law under penalty of death. It appears,
along with two other rosary meditations, in the
second edition of a book entitled *The Societie of the
Rosarie* published in c. 1596. The book was
compiled by Henry Garnet, the superior of the
Jesuits in England, who was martyred in 1606, his
head placed on a pole near London Bridge. Terse,
powerful, but with lyric beauty, the old meditation is
still very prayable.

It cannot be determined with certainty from the text
whether Garnet himself composed this meditation in
Latin, then translated it into English, or whether he
translated it from some other Latin source. The title
page of *The Societie of the Rosarie* says the book
was "written in Italian, by the Reverend Father
Lucas Pinelli of the Society of Jesus." This is, of
course, a pseudonym to protect the author. But there
actually was an Italian Jesuit named Luca Pinelli,
and Garnet had translated and published some of his

work earlier. Then the scriptural meditation is introduced by the words "taken out of the Italian book of the Rosarie". This may be to protect the author, a ruse of his humility, or actually so. One of the other meditations in *The Societie of the Rosarie* is clearly from another source: a lovely version of Dominic of Prussia's meditation which was first published at Trier in c. 1415.

It would not surprise me if a sixteenth century Italian book on the rosary were discovered someday containing just this meditation in Latin. It would also not surprise me if no such book were ever discovered. But whoever first composed the meditation, it makes compelling praying. Read the verse in bold type before each Our Father and the subsequent verses before each Hail Mary. (The spelling has been modernized somewhat, and the interspersed Latin version has been left out, but otherwise the meditation is the same as it appeared in 1596. The inconsistencies in the spelling, e.g. Mary/Marie, mysterie/Misterie, are in the original.)

Some Old Advice
for Praying the Rosary

The best advice for Praying the Rosary that I have
ever seen appeared in a book published
anonymously in 1598 at an illegal press in England
during the persecution. The book is entitled *A
Methode, to Meditate on the Psalter, or Great
Rosarie of Our Blessed Ladie: With a Preface in the
Defence and Comendation of It*. Here is the advice,
in verse, exactly as it appeared in 1598, except the
spelling has been modernized somewhat:

1. First, not for course pre-fixed thus,
   a better thought to shun:
   For when you have what you desire,
   what would you more have done?

2. Next, shake superfluous insight off,
   from the understanding still:
   And so betake this charge unto
   affections of the will.

3. The third advice, is that the will
   be not too vehement:
   To seek for sobs and tears by force,
   but quiet and content.

4. The fourth, to use attention due,
   eschewing each extreme:
   Too much hurts too much, too little more,
   the best rests in the mean.

5. The fifth, not to dismay yourself,
   although devotion fail:
   But patiently expect the end,
   in hope you may prevail.

6. The sixth, not to be over short,
   for dew doth bring small gain:
   The barren soil which should be soused
   with lusty showers of rain.

7. The seventh, Gods visitings to take,
   as quietly as you may:
   For man which shuns God, seeking him
   May seek him, and have nay.

In the seven points which follow I have attempted to render this advice in modern terms:

1. Be open when you pray the rosary. Let God lead you into new dimenstions of it. Why are you praying the rosary anyway?

2   Forget what you have been taught about the rosary: make it your own.

3. Relax. Don't bring anything to the rosary; just bring yourself.

4. Pay attention. But not *too much* attention. Some of those distractions may be trying to tell you something.

5. Don't let yourself get discouraged. Be patient until the rosary reveals itself.

6. Don't rush through the rosary. Savour it, linger over it. Let it rain.

7. And don't freak out if you actually get in touch with God.

The
Joyfull Misteries

I

Contemplations upon the First Joyfull Misterie

The Angel Gabriel was sent of God into a citie of Galilee, called Nazareth.

To a Virgin espoused to a man, whose name was Joseph, of the house of David; and the Virgins name was Marie.

And the Angel being entred in, saide unto her, Haile full of grace, our Lord is with thee: Blessed art thou among women.

Who having heard, was troubled at his saying, and thought what manner of Salutation this should be.

And the Angel said to her, feare no Mary, for thou hast found grace with God.

Behold thou shalt conceive in thy womb, and shalt beare a sonne, and thou shalt call his name Jesus.

He shall be great, and shall be called the Son of the most High.

Our Lord God shall give him the Seat of David his father: and he shall reigne in the house of Jacob for ever, and of his kingdom there shall be no end.

And Marie saide to the Angel, How shall this be done, because I know not man?

And the Angel answeringe, saide to her, The holie Ghost shall come upon thee, and the power of the most high, shall overshadow thee. And therfore also that which of thee shall be borne holy, shall be called the sonne of God.

And Mary said to the Angel, behold the handmaid of our Lord, be it done to me according to thy word.

II

*Contemplations upon
the Second Joyfull Misterie*

**And Marie rising up in those days,
went unto the hill-countrie with speed.
into a citie of Juda.**

And she entred into the house of Zacharie, and saluted Elisabeth.

And it came to passe, as Elisabeth heard the salutation of Mary.

The infant did leape in her wombe.

And Elisabeth was replenished with the holy Ghost: and she cried out with a loude voice, and said.

Blessed are thou among women and blessed is the fruite of thy wombe.

And whence is this to me, that the mother of my Lord doth come to me?

For behold as the voice of thy salutation sounded in mine eares, the infant in my womb did leape for joy.

And blessed art thou that believed, because those things shall be accomplished, that were spoken to thee by our Lord.

And Mary said, my soule doth magnifie our Lord, and my spirite hath rejoyced in God my Saviour.

And Marie taried with her about three monthes: and she returned into her house.

III

Contemplations upon the Third Joyfull Misterie

There came forth an edict from Cesar Augustus, that the wholle world should be enrolled.

And Joseph also went up from Galilee, out of the citie of Nazareth into Bethlem.

To be enrolled with Marie his espoused wife, that was with childe.

And it came to passe, when they were there, her days were fully come that she should be delivered. And she brought forth her first begotten sonne.

And swadled him in clothes, and laid him downe in a manger: because there was not place for them in the Inne.

And there were in the same countrie, shepheards watching, and keeping the night watches over their flocke.

And the Angel of our Lord saide to them. Behold I Evangelize to you great joy. Because this day is borne to you a Saviour, which is Christ our Lord, in the citie of David.

And suddenly there was with the Angel, a multitude of the heavenly army, praising God, and saying.

Glorie in the highest to God: and in earth peace to men of goodwill.

And the Shepheards came with speed: And they found Marie and Joseph, and the Infant laide in the manger.

And the Shepheards returned, glorifying and praising God in all things that they had heard and seene, as it was said to them.

IV

Contemplations upon the Fourth Joyfull Misterie

After the days were fully ended of the purification of Marie.

They caried Jesus into Jerusalem, to present him to our Lord.

And behold there was a man in Jerusalem, named Simeon, and this man was just and religious, expecting the consolation of Israel.

And he had received an answere of the Holy Ghost, that he shoulde not see death, unless he saw first the Christ of our Lord.

And Simeon came in spirit into the Temple.

And when his parents brought in the child Jesus, Simeon tooke him into his armes, and blessed God, and said.

Now thou doest dismiss thy servant O Lord, in peace.

Because mine eyes have seene, thy Salvation, which thou hast prepared before the face of all peoples.

And his father and mother were marveling upon these things, which were spoken concerning him.

And there was Anne a Prophetesse, and she spake of him to all that expected the redemption of Israel.

And after they had whollie done all things, they returned into their citie Nazareth.

V

Contemplations upon the Fifth Joyfull Misterie

When Jesus was twelve yeres old, his parents went up into Jerusalem according to the custome of the festivall day.

And having ended the days, when they returned, the childe Jesus remained in Jerusalem, and his parents knew it not.

And thinking that he was in the company, they came a days journey, and sought him among their kinfolke and acquaintance.

And not finding him, they returned into Jerusalem, seeking him.

And after three days, they found him in the temple, sitting in the middes of the Doctors, hearing them, and asking them.

And all were astonished that heard him, upon his wisdome and answers.

And the mother of Jesus saide to him, Sonne why hast thou so done to us?

Behold thy father and I sorrowing did seeke thee.

And he said to them, what is it that you sought me? did you not know, that I must be about those things, which are my fathers?

And they understood not the word that he spake unto them.

And he went downe with them and came to Nazareth, and was subject to them.

And Jesus proceeded in wisdome and age, and grace with God and men.

The
Sorowfull Misteries

VI

Contemplations upon the First Sorowfull Misterie

Jesus went forth with his Disciples, beyond the torrrent Cedron, where was a Garden, into the which he entered.

And when he was come to the place, he said to them, pray, lest yee enter into temptation.

The spirite indeed is prompt, but the flesh weake.

And he was pulled away from them a stones cast: and kneeling he prayed, saying, Father if thou wilt, transferre this chalice from me.

But yet not my will, but thine be done.

He went againe, and prayed, saying the selfe same word thy will be done.

And when he was risen up from prayer, he found his Disciples sleeping for pensiveness.

And he saith to Peter, Simon sleepest thou? couldest thou not watch one houre with me?

And being in an agonie, he prayed the longer.

And his sweat became as droppes of blood, trickling downe upon the earth.

And there appeared to him an Angel from heaven strengthening him.

VII

Contemplations upon the Second Sorowfull Misterie

The ministers of the Jewes apprehended Jesus, and bound him.

And the men that held him, mocked him, beating him.

You have presented unto me this man, as averting the people.

And beholde I examing him before you, have founde no cause in this man of those things wherein you accuse him.

No, nor Herod neither, for I sent you to him, and behold, nothing worthie of death is done to him.

I will chasten him therefore, and dismisse him.

Then therefore Pilate tooke Jesus and scourged him.

Pilate seeing that he nothing prevailed, taking water he washed his hands before the people.

And saide, I am innocent of the blood of this just man.

Then he released to them Barrabas,

And having scourged Jesus, delivered him unto them for to be crucified.[1]

---

1. In the original text, one Hail Mary verse is missing. I have divided the last verse in two.

VIII

*Contemplations upon
the Third Sorowfull Misterie*

**The Presidents soldiers tooke Jesus
into the Palace.**

And gathered together unto him, the wholle band.

And stripping him, put a scarlet cloke about him.

And platting a crowne of thornes, put it upon his head.

And put a reed in his right hand.

And spitting upon him, they tooke the reed, and smote his head.

And bowing the knee before him, they mocked him, saying, Haile Kinge of the Jewes.

And certaine beganne to spitt upon him, and to cover his face, and to beate him with buffets, and to say unto him, Prophecie etc.

And the servantes gave him blowes.

Jesus therfore went forth carrying the crowne of thornes, and the purple vestment.

And Pilate saithe to them, Loe the man.

IX

Contemplations upon the Fourth Sorowfull Misterie

Then therefore Pilate delivered Jesus unto them for to be crucified.

And they tooke Jesus, and led him forth.

And Jesus bearing his owne Crosse, he went forth.

And going, they found a man of Cyrene named Simon: him they forced to take up his Crosse.

And there followed him a great multitude of people, and of women, which bewailed and lamented him.

But Jesus turning to them, said, Daughters of Jerusalem, weepe not upon me.

But weepe upon your selves, and upon your children.

For behold the days shall come wherin they will say:

Blessed are the barren, and the wombes that have not borne, and the pappes that have not given sucke.

If in the greene wood they do these things, in the dry what shall be done?

And there were led also, other two malefactours with him to be executed.

And they came into the place that is called Golgotha, which is the place of Calvarie.

X

Contemplations upon the Fifth Sorowfull Misterie

And after they came to the place which is called Calvarie; there they crucified him.

Then were crucified with him, two thieves: one on the right hand, and one on the left.

And Jesus said, Father forgive them, for they knowe not what they do.

And Jesus said to the thiefe, Amen I say to thee: this day thou shalt be with me in Paradise.

And he said to his mother: woman behold thy sonne.

After that, he saith to the Disciple, Behold thy mother.

Jesus cried with a mightie voice, saying: My God, my God, why hast thou forsaken me?

That the scripture might be fulfilled, he saith, I thirst.

Jesus therfore when he had taken the viniger, said, It is consummate.

And Jesus crying with a loude voice, said, Father, into thy hands I commend my spirite.

And Jesus againe crying with a mightie voice, yielded up the ghost.

The
Glorious Misteries

XI

Contemplations upon the First Glorious Misterie

**Marie Magdalene and
Marie of James, and Salome
bought spices, that coming they
might annoint Jesus.**

And behold there was made a greate earthquake: And for feare, the watchmen were frighted, and became as dead.

An Angel of our Lorde descended from heaven: and rolled backe the stone and sat upon it.

And the Angel said to the women, feare not you, you seeke Jesus that was crucified: he is not here, for he is risen, as he said.

Come and see the place, where our Lord was laid.

But go, tell his Disciples and Peter, that he is risen.

Behold he goeth before you into Galilee: there you shall see him, as he told you.

And they went forth quickly out of the monument with feare and great joy, running to tell his Disciples.

And behold Jesus met them, saying, all haile.

But they came near and tooke hold of his feet, and adored him.

Then Jesus said to them, feare not, go tell my brethren that they go into Galilee, there they shall see me.

XII

*Contemplations upon
the Second Glorious Misterie*

**He showed him selfe alive
after his passion in many arguments.**

For fortie days appearing to his Apostles, and speaking of the kingdome of God.

They therefore that were assembled, asked him, saying, Lord, whether at this time wilt thou restore the kingdome to Israel.

But he said to them: It is not for you to knowe times or moments, which the Father hath put in his owne power.

But you shall be witnesses unto me in Jerusalem, and in all Jewrie, and Samaria, and even to the utmost of the earth.

And when he had said these things, in their sight he was elevated: and a cloud received him out of their sight.

God ascended in exceeding joy, and our Lord in sound of trumpet.[1]

And when they beheld him going into heaven, behold two men stood beside them in white garments.

And said, ye men of Galilee, why stand you looking into heaven?

This Jesus which is assumpted from you into heaven, shall so come, as you have seen him going into heaven.

And it came to passe while he blessed them, he departed from them, and was caried into heaven.

---

1. This is Psalm 46:6.

XIII

Contemplations upon the Third Glorious Misterie

Then they returned to Jerusalem, from the mount that is called Olivet, which is by Jcrusalem, distant a Sabeths journey.

And when they were entred in, they went up into an upper chamber, where abode Peter and John, James and Andrew,

Philippe and Thomas, Bartholomew and Mathew, James of Alphaeus and Simon Zelotes, and Jude of James.

All these were persevering with one mind in prayer, with the women, and Mary the mother of Jesus.

And when the days of Pentecost were accomplished, they were all together in one place.

And suddenly there was made a sound from heaven, as of a vehement wind comming.

And it filled the wholle house, where the Apostles were sitting.

And there appeared to them, parted tonges as it were of fire.

And it sat upon every one of them.

And they were all replenished with the holy Ghost.

And they beganne to speake with diverse tongues, according as the holy Ghost gave them to speake.

But they going forth, preached every where: our Lord working withall, and confirming the word with signs that followed.

XIV

*Contemplations upon
the Fourth Glorious Misterie*

**Arise, make haste my love, my dove,
my beautifull and come.**

For now the winter is past, the shower is gone, and ceased.

Show me thy face, let thy voice sound in my eares.

For thy voice is sweet, and thy face comely.

What is she, that ascended through the desert like to a streame of perfumed smoke, arising from odoriferous gummes of Myrrhe and Incense, and all maner of sweete powder of the perfumer?

What is she, that increaseth as the break or dawning of the day?

Faire as the moon, pure as the sun, terrible as an armie set in battle array.

My love thou art altogether beautiful, and no spot is in thee, come from Libanus my spouse, come from Libanus, come thou shalt be crowned.

I will go up into the Date tree, and I will take the fruites thereof.

Thou hast sustained my right hand, and thou hast lead me according to thy will, and thou hast received me with glorie.[1]

Marie assumpted into heaven, the Angels rejoyce, and praising, they blesse our Lord.[2]

---

1. This is Psalm 72:23-4.
2. This is not scripture. No source for it is given in the original.

XV

Contemplations upon the Fifth Glorious Misterie[1]

King Salomon arose to meet with Bathsheba his mother, and he adored her, and did sit upon his Throne.

---

1. The sources for the passages in this mystery are given in the Latin original as 2 Kings 3, 2 Kings 3, 2 Kings 3, Judith 15, Esther 2, Psalm 44, Psalm 20, Sirach 45, Isaiah 62, Ezekiel 16, and Revelation 12.

And a Throne was placed for the mother of the King, who did sit at his right hand.

And the King saide to her: Demand O mother: for it is not lawfull that I disdain thy face.

Thou art the glorie of Jerusalem, thou art the joy of Israel, thou art the honor of our people.

The King loved her above all women, and put the diademe of his kingdome upon her head.

The Queene stood at his right hand in a Clothing of gold, embroidered with variety.

He put on her head a crowne of precious stone.

A crowne of gold upon her mitre, in which was engraved, Sanctitie to our Lord.

And the bridegroome shall rejoyce at his spouse, and thy God shall rejoyce at thee.

I have arayed thee with an ornament, and I have put

bracelets on the wristes of thy handes, and a chaine about thy necke. And I have put a jewell on thy fore head, and earings in thy eares, and a most comely crowne on thy head.

A great signe appeared in heaven: a woman clothed with the sun, and the moon under her feet, and on her head a crowne of twelve stars.